silent ambiguity

poetry by

Daniel Luke Nunley

authorHOUSE®

AuthorHouse™
1663 Liberty Drive
Bloomington, IN 47403
www.authorhouse.com
Phone: 1-800-839-8640

First published by AuthorHouse 10/13/2009

ISBN: 978-1-4389-9256-3 (sc)

Printed in the United States of America
Bloomington, Indiana

This book is printed on acid-free paper.

Contents

wandering romance in the bleakest wood

wandering romance in the bleakest wood
her bold brown eyes blossomed and descended
like the leaves of autumn
and liquefied the spirits of his fervor
as his heart fell before her fragile vessels
the little boy in his coat, standing there
in the bleakest wood
her abstruse eyes...opening and closing
watching, ignoring
the little boy in his coat, standing there
in the bleakest wood
she turns away, and his heart goes after her
but his legs are paralyzed, unsure
and he stands there in his coat
locked in his world in the bleakest wood
the rattling of his passions upset the very
oxygen that he breathes
and he chokes
his eyes watering, his breathing toxic
everything becoming poisonous
but he stands there in his coat
and doesn't chase the freedom in her smile
the air that she breathes
he just stands there in his coat and
waves after her, breathing his inky fumes
surrounded in the bleakest wood and
the most senseless scenery

the girl with the brown eyes so abstruse
reaches down into the forest and
pulls him by his arm
they embrace
and he feels her lips against his
if only in his heart, he is in heaven
no longer surrounded by the mess he created
no longer in the senseless scenery
no longer the tree in the wood
standing still, unmoved
wrapped up in that coat of bark
he breathes in her light and
freedom envelops him
if only in his heart they are kissing
but his eyes, so abstruse to her,
his hazel eyes only see the washed
out colors of green and brown and black
so they absolve into gray
as he retreats into his world
the little boy in his coat
standing there afraid
standing alone in the bleakest wood
a chorus begins the lament...

clouds and we fall

i wonder if an
angel without wings is
still beautiful
but i'd bet they're ugly
probably disfigured like
a fallout victim that
didn't find a shelter
or some poor soul
who got beat up on the
golden streets by
a gang of disciples
in the moonlight i
see them with their
perfect faces and
their eyes so soft
like they're holding
grace in midnight
wandering the hills
and the elysian fields
with the dews and
the birches and the
honey on my tongue
this is all before the
bomb drops and the
air gets white and
the shadows burn to
the ground
where the sun sets beyond
the crystal seas and
the gates of pearl
and gemstones shimmer
and wink at me
is where they dropped
the big one and
everything faded

quirk the quality

my god, i'm filthy
and i can't justify it
my mind feels like
it's been trampled
by the boots of
a thousand soldiers
evil ones
with pointed heels and
forked tongues
and i just stand there
like a tree being cut
i don't defend myself
i'm helpless
these Nazis saw off
my limbs and insects
and creatures chew and
eviscerate my bark
demon children laugh
at my misfortunes
and satan plays a
guitar with a certain
number of strings that
i can't count
it's an evil sound
probably in phrygian
although i could never tell
for all my knowledge
i'm fairly stupid when
it comes to these things
the difference between normal
and abnormal
i only ever saw good and evil
only ever felt angelic
and demonic
yeah, i'm weird
and filthy and they're
all going to destroy
me for it

parade

pineapple dreams and
banana sunsets
wild world of ticklish
pumpkin seeds and
dancing kiwis
strawberry delights the
pear is unusually popular
its american pie
orange tornados and
lemon hurricanes
the rain is lime
it's the parade of the century
the grand marshal mr. honeydew
is tossing grapes to the crowd
there is a raffle for
a great big cantaloupe
star fruit can-can and
peach motorcades
the apricots are jealous
the lesser fruits!
navels and tangerines
oh, and the tangelos
tag along, invisible
the grapefruit savior
with its ruby red
sweetness it's the
only hope for the
strange man
oh, the lesser fruits!
so insignificant their
plea so tinny their voices
perhaps only the god apple
can determine their fate

haunted

what visions haunt my spirit
as i lie in wake this night
a sleepless fever boils
my dancing shadows
in this moment
i seek redemption
the scars never healing
revealing the past
and a liquid evil snakes
its way through my blood
of all the stars and
angels in heaven
not one can cast down the
sorrow that feeds upon me
this demon grapples with
corruption upon my back
all my flesh is ripped away
and all my tears are
shed in vain
for on this day the
innocence died
strangled by the rope
of its confusion
so i lower myself
into its grave
will no one save me
from this pit?
will he not save me
from the trench of
my despair?

darkness

a blank stare cast upon me
i returned it without expression
as the anger and hurt left my body
i watched all around me slowly
fade to black
no plain course visible
i struggled about
on my knees
and all around me reduced itself
to rubble
allowing the evil
to consume them
a hush fell over the air
a pause for remembrance
but a streaking arrow shattered
the silence
weighted
driven by sorrow and
by love
the tepid sea once again
began to scream and boil
the wind shrieked
and drove back the vessel of courtesy
imposing itself to power the
will of action
but all remained black

it's some kind of drug

the lips on that whore
they're sickeningly sweet
but diseased
viral
and every time we kiss
she sucks the life
out of me
gives me a sickness
some infection that takes
hold of me and
shakes me like the
wife of a drinker
she disgusts me
her appetite is
never satiated
she always hungers
always lingers
always gives me that
paralyzing stare
slut that she is
sticking her feet in
the air and
breathing smoke in my face
i'm completely dominated by
her, and all her
garbage
addicted to that high
her moans and groans
her writhing
and that paralyzing stare
that damned stare
i think i'll just
look away
drink this bourbon
and read Proverbs

in cases of

she looked into my eyes
and asked me why
never speaking
but i could hear her
and everything was flashing
crashing
one time when she was
on her hands and knees
and i pulled her hair
and she yelled
her blonde hair draped
over her breasts
as she overtook me
straddling
there was an explosion
and she screamed
and another girl
blonder still
as we sat in a church
next to the baptism pool
and it was dark
she cried and told me she loved me
but i did nothing
let her suffer in anxious ecstasy
and the blood rushed south
as if gravity demanded it
filling up my temptation
raising and showing off my desires
then another one on my floor
laying sideways, naked
looking up at me, asking me
writhing around with her hand

past her naval
and we dove into layers
and she released herself on me
as i her
and we held each other for a while
and i kissed her tenderly
laying sideways, naked
another clawed at my feet
removal of clothes was a science
looking up at me, asking me
writhing around with her hand
between her thighs
and i said i should read
my bible
and i realized the futility
of all of it
and hated my position
but still we search
and release our inhibitions with
each other
we hurt afterwards
but the intensity calls
us backward
right back in the layers
and she lies sideways on
my floor
my hands upon her chest
her hand between my legs, grasping me
and we search for the answers
inside ourselves

tagalong

yeah, he's a backup plan
a contingency
i imagine it's like a
slap in the face
his phone never rings
never chimes
and his arrival is
always greeted with surprise
but it's cold and
awkward
like a naked child
he could give all he
has and still the
greeting cards would not come
that phone would sustain
the silence that buries
his mind in his bowels
and still he is not welcome
not by the melodies and
the presence no
not by the hands that
he extends like the bird
spreading its plumage
and showing its beauty
so why shouldn't it be proud
between the lonesome and
the bored and the depraved
and the ignorant he sleeps
like something either pathetic
or simply exhausted
my, oh my he's a sight
and he stands out which
is just really not what we
want
you see we've gotta blend
like the popular crowd and

the compromised and the bigots
you see it's just weird
and you know we gotta relate so
dont blame us
make him change
sure, he'll just adjust to
fit that mold and squeeze right
into that little spot between
the rest of you and smile
because he's plastic now
and doesn't have anything
interesting to say
hey, it's not a commentary
or the ramblings of the misunderstood
but it could be significant to
someone and that's what he's
wanting
just looking for a soul to touch
and he'll place the
ad on his face and stir
the paint with his hands and
maybe he could reach the sky and
make a collage that
you all can admire and
then they'll cherish him
he's not plotting and
not seeking acceptance but
still
your indifference reveals your
shroud and he wants to disrobe
you like the girls you
want to handle
you can be a heartbreak with
your excuses and you know your
eyes can't lie to him
but he's not plotting and
not seeking acceptance but
just wants you to pick up
the phone and send him some
good cheer

puzzle pieces

your simplistic perplexity
betrays the misery behind
your plastic eyes

the symphony pauses
apprehensive
fearful of
the starless flames

my artist virtuosity
paints this masterpiece of
reality
my words, of course
guided

and all your doubt
becomes clear

i assimilate

my crystal intentions
once muddied
become beautiful again

as your world crumbles
i assimilate
and take your place
before the symphony

i assimilate

silent ambiguity

this place is destroying itself
what is the value of the truth
if no one cares to tell it
yeah everybody just wants to lie
it's more interesting more fun
its theater
everything is about jealousy and
sex and lies lies lies but
no one will admit it
its taboo it's all taboo but
everyone does it and its taboo
shut up
transparency
thats what we need
but everybody is just hiding
all the girls take off their
clothes and spread their legs
for bastards and all these guys
are just morons and manipulators and
uncultured
and the double standard is wrong
but it's probably just jealousy
hey its taboo and its taboo but
everyone does it and you do too
so shut up
transparency
thats what you need
i know you're looking for the
truth but i won't give it to you
because you dont care and you dont
care to tell it
you take your clothes off and
spread your legs for liars and morons
and manipulators and bastards and
the uncultured
you just want to lie and have sex
its more interesting more fun
its taboo and you feel grown up
shut up
i'll just sit in
silent ambiguity
and let you destroy yourself

may 24 6:15 a.m.

the morning brings dewish delights
as a welcome to the fatigued
the saturated warmth the bleakness
of striking fire
awkward praises of silly petulance
standing like gods over
camp fires littered by
a nighttime expression
realizations revelations of
utter simplicity hidden by
veils of wooded moon lights
and starry diseases fresh
like a child they welcome
the incredible gift like
the morning that welcomes them
with dewish delights
sunny dispositions amidst the
tragedy of hearts broken in
mirrored cloud mists windows of
eye colored persuasions the iris
of jesus surrounding a porthole
to the soul
the kingly chorus proclaims
trapped between soiled sheets of
adulterous desires and shame of
the whore in the darkness molded
of grey now touched boldly by
that creator with a heart for
the cancerous sincerely and forever yours
the poet of devilish defiance

the immortal one

i walked the silent hills
of the cemetery
a clear afternoon
sunny and temperate
the breeze rustling
the mournful leaves
pressing them onward
guiding them among the dead
the sun glinted off the memorials
the headstones
the statues of listless immortality
staring forever quiet
upon the departed
the beings of ceaseless surrender
and the ravens circled above
clinging to the branches
of the failing trees
their wretched limbs stretching
ever forth into eternity
an eternity with no reprieve
i heard the crow cry
and it was fitting
i lifted my eyes
and there i saw a waterfall
small, but substantial in
and of itself
it emptied into a shallow pool
filled with the tiny minnows
and the crawfish
and the birches lingered out
over the water
among the banks, the lilies
in their simplicity
bent ever towards the sun
and the water skimmers
the tiny things sitting
on the stillness

and the snails and every
little creature
the dragonflies and the snakes
everything at once a beauty
and an omen
reminding me that i sat
amongst those that had passed
it was then that i saw it
a deer, pretty and elegant
it's gaze was tender
and it looked right at me
i felt that question
inside of me
the one that i always hear
and i looked back at
her for an answer
but she only stared at me
and then danced among the
markers, the tombstones
the dead
ceaselessly joyful
indifferently destructive
amazingly serene
and passively ignorant
i could only watch her go
as i sat among the departed
and they cried
but the richweeds groped
at my ankles and i
raised my head
observing what lay before me
on top of the waterfall
i looked down at the field
filled with memory
and the headstones went quiet
and i knew
there was a lot of life in death
sitting among the brush
and the blue azures

be

we are worlds apart
so distant
you're like a whirlwind
and i am the sun
i am beauty
and filth
but so are you
yet you are more beautiful
and delicate like the rain
more powerful than
the oceans
as mysterious as
the dancing clouds
rain on me
i am alive
i am clean
we are
and we can
be

txtributestlin

that beauti&ful man"
       estlinwas
his   name
i could probably write:him a
tribute
like something *crazy^ in form
because i've got my favorite things he's written but
             i dontreallyknow how
   i should
try to pay himrespect
               i'll use
my tiny hands

it's the decades and the timeless

yeah, the 20's were roaring
two decades later and our
boys are dying in a
harbor of pearls
but they were more like lambs

then you had the
american dream
television appeared
and everyone watched
and it was important, we thought

then there was vietnam and
we tried to be heroes
and everyone was all pissed
off and burned their clothes
worshipped mother nature
and human things

the little kids in
mother naija starved
and our sisters in russia
stood in lines for their
milk and bread
and over here a soup can
is "pop culture"

there were problems in
south africa and rwanda but
this time we decided the world
didn't need us
and we made our money worthless

ours was the society of
show and pomp
everybody wants to be the
nu thang
and we're ignorant

yeah, we'll fight a dictator
and tear down a wall
but things crumble anyway
and we build another barrier
inside ourselves
and we can't face it

not even as a country
while one person can stand
in tienimen square in front of
a tank and we're cowards
but we're so important
like a nu thang
and we make the scene

yeah, sometimes i wonder when
the seven years will end
or if they've begun
or maybe we're just
caught in the middle
no...no...
here comes the twilight

clay

i am a miry clay
shapeless, formless
but my love is strong enough
to melt the stars
in my despondency i
impose upon myself a
destitution
i have nothing
i am nothing
but he is everything
he is gracious enough to
pick me up
this shadowy mass of clay
and wash away the filth
creating the fragile vessel
his messenger
what i was always meant
to be
for that
is how he saw me
beautiful
fragile
and his
for i am nothing
and he is everything

part time prophet, full time by audience

criminal
that is what they call me
self-involved and
without conscious
falsifying
denying
hypnotizing
like a rapist
i am taking away
your identity
your peace of mind
like a murderer
like a murderer
im taking away
your very life
criminal
that is my name
i sit behind bars
that have been crafted
for me
i sit behind bars
that have been crafted
by my own hands
i'm a sinner
a liar
and the whores
always follow
you think i'm your troubadour
and it makes me sick
i'm not a soothsayer
i'm not your placemat
criminal
that is who i am
just another false messiah
so gather together
i am just like you
a part time prophet
and you, my audience
long to be touched
never mind the poets and painters
i'll just sit here
and drink my london fog

what i am lacking is motivation

just a pretender
eating my day old chinese food
delivery pizzas and
green tea
watching reruns
writing poetry
thinking i'm important
smoking cigars
and popping pills
calling whores and
abusing myself
acting prophetic
making epic the
mundane and the contrived
reading shakespeare and
yeats, william blake
and michael crichton
i hear longfellow in
my sleep and daydream
about fitzgerald
and hemingway
i try to gather myself
among these men, these
writers
try to make myself
important and talented
but all i have is
spirit
i'm talentless
listless
stupid

and the bourbon just
echoes it
even through the soothing
the burning proves it
no amount of saline and
plastic could ever
fix the ugliness that i
possess
but there is one who can
maybe i'll throw away
this kentucky shine
move to a monastery
and embrace the truth
only by his grace
may i be saved
he lets me walk the
streets of baltimore and
london
the alleys of edinburgh
and the freeways of los angeles
the villas of tuscany and
the historic streets of
philadelphia that i call home
i think i'll move away
move to tibet or somewhere
so i can train and
meditate
and let his grace envelop me
in the fog of the world that
i've been embracing

the pornographic press

i wish i could destroy that cosmopolitan
sitting there on the magazine rack
pushing its filthy brand of
adultery down our throats

i wish i could take all the sex
sitting there on the magazine rack
and dissolve it in the inky blood
of my pen
dissolve it
and let the mud of its
decadence settle to the
bottom of society's looking glass

then everyone could see
how disgusting it is
everyone could see the vile
fragility, the putrid
wretchedness of what is
sitting there on the magazine rack

i wish i could take all the candid
celebrity trash
sitting there on the magazine rack
and crumble it in my hands
until all the pathetic
broken pop stars
can't be heard moaning
and the celebrities cry
for reprieve
their screams drowned out
lost inside the flashing bulbs
lost to the soulless paparazzi
lost to the magazine rack

the pornographic press feed
their aphrodisiacs into the ears
and eyes of a public derelict
of morality
the pornographic press sells
their sex to our little children
our adolescents
we all forget our self worth

i'm so sick of the pornographic press
putting their trash on the magazine rack

i'm so sick of everyone
living their lives
on the magazine rack

i wish we'd all stop
sitting there on the magazine rack

the night before he rises

its 2:43 and i
can't sleep and its
so dark but i have
my television on
i'm just so tired
right now but can't
sleep and i'm really
in a tragic mood with
these thoughts and
dreams crowding up
in my head like some
sort of wordy mob
and i hate it
tomorrow is easter
and i think i'll
rise feeling about
like that
if i ever sleep
maybe my door will
open up like a
stone in front of
a tomb and i'll
walk out like a
miracle
if i was dead i
really don't remember
but i just feel like it
my eyes are beginning
to sink and my mind
is beginning to wander
i'm a mess, i know it
and i'm reaching out
to find some hand
to grab
the only one that
reaches is some king
but he's got scars

on his wrists
i really don't know
i keep on making
my own little culture and
i want to have this style
people call me
unconventional and
i like it
social backlash and those
false messiahs
a bunch of so-called
"christians" who
break their commandments
and i'm one of them
the mundane and i'm
stagnant, misunderstood
it's my excuse anyway
poets and painters
lovers and stairways
the chapels and the
confessional booth
i'll be on my knees
but you won't find me
there
i'll be in my own world
disappearing
and looking for salvation
yeah, there are scars on
his wrists
but i'm so filthy that
i can't see them

the artist

you just love the audience
all the screamers and dancers
but you're not feeding them
you don't know what they need
just a little boy
pretending to be a man

playing your 5-stringed guitar

you're hungry too
but you tiptoe around the obvious
skirt the reality of your
despondent outlook
you just smile and sit on the stage

playing your 5-stringed guitar

just keep smiling at those faces
just keep flirting with the floozies
just stay on the stage
and fake another smile

playing your 5-stringed guitar

simple kentucky

the weather there is
great, yeah
and there's a lot to do
the cityscapes and
the beaches
downtown and the
historic districts
from fullerton to
the hills
yeah, from 90210 to
hollywood and vine
its where i'm going
i'm heading out west
feeling like a pioneer
but something keeps
calling me
crying, wailing
beckoning me
the kentucky plains
shout for me to stay
their majesty now
apparent, where before
one would see the
destruction of the strip
mines, the coke plants
and the steel mills
the industries and
the smokestacks clear
and i see the beauty of
the kentucky plains
the majestic hills of
Eastern Appalachia
the hospitality and

the kinship
the passion and
the morality
i remember the springtime
in ashland
the summers that were just
too hot, and the unsightly
farmers tan that i brandished
the blessing of the perfect
autumn, with the trees
in display, fully colorized
and showing
the late-night music shows
and summer motion
churches every two blocks
and the coffee shops
worship on sundays and
wednesdays, dining out
with friends, goofing off
talking jesus and "tool time"
the dinners at home, mashed potatoes
chicken and dumplings
and the peach cobblers
ale-8-1
even though we never
called it that
the "1" was for outsiders
wrestlemania parties and
watching raw on mondays
sitting on the bench outside
the home and listening
to the sound of the traffic
all kentucky and ohio drivers
who think my street is Talledega
the winter with 3 feet
of snow
the one time they pulled
me behind that car and down

the hill
getting home at 3 and
going to work at 4
the honest living
and the dirt
going to the movies
and the mall
sitting outside in the park
next to that misshapen pond
the bats whizzing past my head
being at peace
on the kentucky plains
but most of all the people
back in kentucky where
manners and God still matter
back in kentucky where
the food is good
back in kentucky where
the paramount sits
back in kentucky where
i played my music
and did my comedy and
lived
back in kentucky
where i grew up
i'm moving out west
to los angeles
but my heart will always
stay back in kentucky
my heart shouts after me
standing atop
the kentucky plains

transcendental

be my eternity
you flawless angel
spread your divine wings
and soar to the peaks of
your perfection
my lust for your gaze
is insatiable
and your glance only
whets my bottomless
appetite for you
touch me, you
fragile creature
you are pristine
and indomitable
let us transcend this
earthly trespass
to touch
the summit of olympus

the beauty behind closed doors

if god could give me the key to one heart
it would be yours
you are so frail, and so strong
and that beauty is astounding
behind the doors that you close
lies the angel hidden beneath
subjecting herself to the whims and
selfish perceptions of the unwise
and the mediocre
convincing herself of breaking free
trying to spread her wings and take flight
while the bastards and deceivers of
the world tie you down with the
chains of a filthy society
you are locked into the rooms of your mind
the horror crawls up your bedpost and
slowly seeps into your skin
where it feeds
and sucks out every last bit of joy
that you had ever begun to hold
for yourself
if god could give me the key to one door
it would be yours
but you're just so fragile
and the masses have clipped your wings to
prevent you from rising above their
selfish pleasures and useless thoughts
it makes you frail
if god could give me the answer to one riddle
it would be you

revolution

it's about time to start a revolution
i told pastor egypt once that it
was soon at hand and
in a way it was, but i didn't
live it
no, i didn't live the revolution
where's the girl with the
pretty hair and the sultry
smile and that educated mind
i'm still looking for her in
the middle of the mob and they're
pretending to start a revolution
but i know they won't live it
no, we never live it
i hear the echoes and the
moaning and the crying with
the motions of the time and
the culture is revolting
but we won't tolerate it
no, we never tolerate change
there's a reverberation around
this town and i'm feeling like
a coin lost in a washing machine
as if i had lost my fortune
and the tide scrubs me clean
rocks me and spins me like
a wurlitzer and i'm getting so
dizzy and sick and i want out
where is the revolution
the lyric of the decade and
the verse of eons and the
place that i run to and
that paradise that i cling to
and fall and reach out for
with my wings melting and

i'll hit the ground
no, my name is not icarus
and i won't live it
no, i won't live for wishful thinking
and my dreams will never mean
anything because they're not
practical
no, i'm not practical
i'm just the opposite
and maybe i want to be european
or something else alien to
all of you because i'm
a stranger, and i'll never change
no, i can't change and i'm strange
yeah, i'm weird and looking at
all these different things
and i'm thinking about the
revolution that's taken hold
of me
and i was right when i told him
the revolution happened soon
after and the revolution was
in me
yeah, i've lived the revolution

what a crazy crush for this stranger

i sometimes dream of
that velvet face of yours
your silk black hair
your glance evokes such passion
you arouse my eyes to a
vapid gaze
as i draw in the light
of your astounding beauty
but my curiosity is not
enough to subjugate the
apprehension that you create
within me
i think i fear you
your eyes
they're like liquid fire
they melt me
i don't have words to
describe you
so just pour over me
and be mine
we'll paint the moon with
our hands
fill the oceans with
our tears
dance the sun into submission
and write a symphony with
our lips
you and i could be
everything
you and i could
be
melt me, baby
and please
let me melt you

the responses are on the mirror

they say it's provocative and
i'm just going for the gut
shock value and sex
like a moron
no sophistication like
sensitive angels i'm
not the normal type
i read cummings a lot and
oscar wilde drinking tea
and coffee like i'm artsy
or thoughtful but i'm
not the normal type, yeah
i can't pretend it either
where's my espresso? i
think i left in london on
the thames
and the wonder of it all
makes me sing hallelujahs
to the king but i can't
see past that dirty woman
and her boa
even when i'm going along
with the crowd i
know i'm not the normal type
i've got the cityscapes and
castles in mind with

the skyline and the roads
of lancashire, i know it's
where i'm from anyway
with that red rose wearing
it around as a corsage and
showing it
i'm proud i know and
i'm not the normal type so
quit reminding me
and we'll look past the
tattoos and the wild hair
and the rambling words and
the musings and my insignificance
and my self-importance
and my self-realization and
all the pieces that i carve
and shine the light
on the art that i wish
to create

the lime green obsession

it's the smile that i never see
the laugh that i never hear
the strawberries of your hair
the freckles on your nose
your eyes after our first kiss
the peaches of your lips
the lime green obsession

your terra-cotta expressions
outline the fragility behind
your grin
that crowd pleaser
the show

that glance of apprehension
when you hope my eyes are
not wandering

you can't even look at me
without turning away

it's the way you wish you
didn't feel
the way that i cant
the long kiss goodbye
that never happened
the lime green obsession

regardless of truth
reality
feelings
and remorse
you have grown from this
so why be childish?
why force immaturity
on yourself?
so embrace that new breath
and grow like you know
you're supposed to

but don't let go
don't ever let go
because it'll never let go
so never let go
never let go
of your lime green obsession

first truth, deception abound the memory

i remember the way you
looked at me that one
night on the bus ride home
how we held hands and
i just gazed into your eyes
and i felt that fire all
over me
my chest was all lit up
and hot blood filled
my ears, as i held
you as close as i
could. and i remember
loving you then, even there
and loving you like i
was crazy. and we didn't
say a word, save one
when i said god had
answered my prayers
you know, it was true
so it makes me wonder
where the fire went
when did that hot light
fade and make me want
something else, something
false, useless, stupid...
and it took so much for
me to learn about you and
what love was and how
i knew i was growing
where did it go?
my dreams of you are

few these days. but when
they come i always wake
up with that heat raging
and hot blood filling my
ears, and i hold
you as close as i
can, if only in my dreams
and the memory of your
peachy smile and your
preciousness and the
tenderness of your lips and
how i know the truth.
and if i had known
it all then and
if i had known it
all then back about
that time
if i had known it
all then i would
be holding you in my
arms right now and
kissing your lips so sweet

the look on her face the night that she knew

so you just realized it tonight
she loved you
you remember seeing
that look on her face
the same one you saw tonight from
some other couple near your dinner table
probably newlyweds or something
that deep, entranced look that
shows her devotion
completely in love with you
you are so stupid
and blind and
despicable
tell me was it worth it
breaking that little
heart for nothing
for a few hours of
life on the other side
was it worth all the
pills the hospital beds
and the blood
was it worth all the hunger and
the yearning and the wailing
and the screaming
hey what good came of it
and you just realized it tonight
you bastard
you are a damned fool and you
always have been
yeah you can talk all about it
and wonder and wish
if you knew then what you know now
and if you knew then
that you were in love and she
loved you so much
so what
its over
yeah it's too late
so quit dreaming and be quiet
you miss her you miss her you miss it all
you missed it
you make me sick

little goddess

my own personal venus
a little goddess
magnetizing, mesmerizing
misinformed
the creation that is tempted
torn from my rib and
presented to me on
a silver cloud like
the linen sheets we
were meant to mess
she lays her head on
my chest and my heart
beats for her
and then the serpent comes
here, child, is the
fruit of knowledge
eat and you will be whole
so my innocence is taken
because she gave hers away
my own personal venus
a little goddess
a little goddess torn
from my rib and
given to me held in
the hand of the almighty
oh, my little baby
my little venus
here, i extend the fruit
of knowledge
the mighty seed of lust
this is my greed
oh, my oath

i give to you my little venus
place your little hand
in mine, i'll pull
the tears from your breast
place your little hand in
mine, goddess
and let me share the
knowledge of life with you
this is my greed
my little venus
lay your head on my chest
my heart beats for you
my little venus
my magnetizing, mesmerizing
misinformed little venus
love, your creator

left the garden

shit this isn't right
ladybug of ignorance
throw away the smiles
the lies the body electric
although i applaud your effort
skeleton of steel and your
little grey lips where
death passes through
miss peach of deep desires
you know you've lost your flavor
your little feet, they carry you far
from your home you little ladybug
you ignorant little thing
with all your divisiveness
naked from the neck down
subtlety, it's your game
baby your freckles, i lied
they're cancer
sorry little ladybug
you're already dead
you ignorant little thing
skeleton of steel and your
bad intentions you know
that's all thats left
i sucked death from your lips
but you little miss peach
little ladybug of ignorance
you hung yourself on the
lines of powder lies
shot your little feet
and they carried you far
from where you should have been
tiny little thing, poor baby
pluck the apathy from your
crest of many colors, the
very rainbow of misdeeds
from what cucumber do you nest
and what little ladybug have
you done with your innocence
shit this isn't right
little ladybug of ignorance
sorry it's time to kill you

discovery

she's dead by the
time the half moon rises
her body is darkness
the fabric of space
shifts around her
there's a solar system
circling her stomach
she grabs the sun
and swallows it
vomits star dust and
supernovas find their
way out the back of her
the galaxies in her eyes
begin to fade
the black holes of
her pupils absorb her
essence every bit
of light she ever held
i come down upon her
and set down the lander
one small step for man
now her body is
my lunar playground
her stare blank
i orbit her everything
the shuttle descends
from the darkness
and licks time from
her birth canal

the wasted words of the forfeited mind

the wasted words of the forfeited mind
they're as useless as regret
something bewildered only stands to
sit down again
with a needle in the eye
there comes a fount of ink and blood
mixing, affixing
it's exotic and perplexing
it's artsy and it's vexing
there's a mind it's annexing
and tests it's strength by its flexing
the hammer is brought
with iron the point is driven home
like a nail
and the rust and blood combine
what has become old is appalling
his words are sprawling
but he's crawling
recalling and mothballing
it's just a god that he's calling
or a whore that he's followed
like a stoning, it's mauling
from every corner he's found
smoking a cigar like he's dignified
he follows the world with his eyes
and pretends to know the mean
he says he makes the scene
claims experience but he's green
feigns contentment like a closet queen
enjoys that which is obscene
all the while they think he's clean
he's been this way since fifteen
he'll never let jesus intervene
he wants his life on the projection screen
wants to be meaner than a wolverine
and his heart beats
like an electrostatic machine
all his playing
it's just routine

from a girl with brown eyes
to one named christine
the faces of his lovers are marked
with betrayal
she always saw
the man with the veil
and he lifts his head in shame
he poses and he's pathetic
searching for fame
there is a jealous deity
whose heart is broken
but the man can't break code
he just stays on the same road
never changing cycle or mode
the transmission's going to explode
he's never remembered and never slowed
he's looking to implode
searching for a soul to corrode
out of ammo, he needs to reload
he wants them to write a horatian ode
of how he broke the barrier
he falters
the words begin to slow
his eyes are pecked
by a carrion crow
being blind he wants to grow
all of this arrived apropos
he no longer believes in his electric glow
his life isn't a shadow show
he's lacked this feeling
since a long time ago
when jesus broke the status quo
he's exposed like on a talk show
but there is freedom in the truth
the wasted words of his forfeited mind
are as useless as his old ways
new words will emerge
and break the walls down
his heart is broken
but jesus is going to repair it

About the Author

Daniel Luke Nunley was born August 3rd, 1990 and currently resides in his hometown of Ashland, Kentucky. Known nationwide as an award winning composer of chamber and new world music, he has also seen critical acclaim in his native state for his achievements in creative videography. He enjoys writing as a pastime, and has begun work on a follow up book of short poems entitled "The Interludes" as well as three novels. He is in the process of relocating to Los Angeles to pursue a career in film. He is a born-again Christian and plays bass guitar for the rock worship group "The Andrew Tyler Band".

Printed in the United States
by Baker & Taylor Publisher Services